MORE *List* YOUR SELF

Other Books by Ilene Segalove and Paul Bob Velick

List Your Self

List Your Creative Self

List Your Self for Parents
(with Gareth Esersky)

Risk Your Self

Other Books by Ilene Segalove

Unwritten Letters

List Your Self for Pregnancy
(with Gareth Esersky)

List Your Self for Kids
(with Charlotte Blumenfeld)

The Write Mood

MORE List YOUR SELF

Listmaking as the Way to Personal Discovery

ILENE SEGALOVE AND PAUL BOB VELICK

Andrews McMeel Publishing
Kansas City

02 03 04 05 06 RDH 10 9 8 7 6 5 4 3 2 1

ISBN: 0-7407-2225-5

Library of Congress Control Number: 2001053588

Book design by Holly Camerlinck

To all those who have placed me on their lists;
There is no way to listmaking. Listmaking is the way.

—*Paul Bob Velick*

To the inventors of lined paper and pencils with erasers.
Thank you for the jump start. And to George.

—*Ilene Segalove*

CONTENTS

INTRODUCTION

List Thy Self, Know Thy Self

A wise old listmaker once said, "To be is to think, and to think is to make lists." The rhyme and reason behind this thought is simple: No matter how we feel or what we do, as long as we are alive, we are thinking, and we are making lists. It's only natural! Lists of plants, lists of parts, lists of ingredients for dinner, and, of course, the never-ending lists of things to do, places to go, and people to see.

Whether we are aware of it or not, our very being is a collection of potential lists. All of us are 24/7 thinking and processing dynamos. The ins and outs and ups and downs of our lives are defined, scripted, and taken for a ride as the result of our listmaking powers.

The deal is, we hardly pay much attention to this urge unless it requires us to get something done. Then, we take all those words floating around in our brains a little more seriously, grab a pen, and jot it all down. Pick up the dry cleaning. Get more dog food. Drop off shoes. Call the accountant. Surely you've made a few dozen or even a few thousand of these to-do lists—lists that smack of productivity and keep our lives running a little smoother. But rarely do these lists leap beyond errands or project management into the realm of lists with a capital "L."

You may have traversed through the original *List Your Self* and uncovered all kinds of exotic information about yourself that you never knew before. With its abundance of provocative list subjects, it probably has your list muscles well in tune. You can, of course, start with either that book or this one, as they both lead you down the path of self discovery. So take the plunge. Pick up the original *List Your Self* or jump right into *More List Your Self*. Either way, you'll be clarifying who you are, what you know, what you want, and how to blaze your trail to a powerful future.

More List Your Self gives you the chance to dive into the giant list pool of your mind and imagination again and asks you to come up with some new superconscious, outside-the-box lists. It's divided into twelve topical chapters that offer all kinds of list adventures from "Your Style" to "Mmmoney," and from "Happy, Healthy, and Wise" to "Culture Club." It gives you the chance to address the breadth and depth of your life experiences in a playful and profound act of self-awareness and mastery.

Perhaps what the wise old listmaker was actually getting at was this: If thinking is part and parcel of who we are, why not engage in the process, use our knowledge, and start calling the shots with more zest and consciousness? Why not start listing and give ourselves the opportunity of becoming more aware of what makes us tick, our values, our dreams, what's important and what's not? *More List Your Self* encourages you to do just that. More than 275 list questions invite you to open your eyes, mind, and heart to deeper levels of self-discovery. It gives you the keys and power to break down the barriers that keep you from living the life you want to live. And it's a direct and honest way to cut through the confusion and aimless spinning we sometimes experience after the challenges of the day.

WHO AM I?

More List Your Self asks you to leap beyond the mundane arena of to-do lists into the outer limits of "Who am I?" It asks you to question, explore, access, assemble, organize, and then write down all of your collected life wisdom, know-how, and personal history. In making your mark, the magic begins. That's truly where the revelatory power of listmaking lies. So take a break, quiet the buzz of your mind, and simply begin making lists.

You can start out very simply. Try "List all of your favorite snack foods." It only takes a second and already you're conjuring up something sweet, something crunchy. But when you put your pen to paper, watch these sensations turn into something tangible, something personal. "Twinkies. Sesame cheddar pretzels. Oh, definitely anything dipped in ranch salad dressing. Dark chocolate. Chocolate. Chocolate." You're on a roll. You list some more. "Cookies. Baby carrots. Blue corn chips." Even a list as seemingly banal as this one creates a portrait of youness. Here's an actual blueprint of your weaknesses and delights!

How about a slightly more profound experiment. "List the greatest loves of your life." "Hmmm . . . gotta go down memory lane to access this long-lost data. Ah, yes, there's Tom from summer camp." Almost instantly scents of honeysuckle and ocean air fill up your senses. "Of course, George and Susie and even Grandpa Philip." It feels good to amble along this path of warmth and connection. It makes you stop and wonder: What is love, really? Whatever happened to all these people? Seeing these significant names lined up, one on top of the other, is a verbal totem to your willingness to have lived and loved.

Our lives span the entire spectrum from ridiculous to sublime. Recording the content gets our juices flowing. After a few lists you can even take a step back from the daily grind to see and appreciate the bigger picture. Somehow, just being asked to make a list creates a mysterious internal shift. You feel energized and clearheaded as you crack open the story of your life. There's so much that's unknown. The best part of discovery is finding the treasures that await you when you walk through that door. So list away!

Don't think. Quick. "List the wildest things you've done in public." You gotta jot down the time you floated in the downtown fountain with those ducks at midnight and the time you twirled a silver baton as you led that marching band dressed in a bikini and heels. But, you might ask yourself, how much of this is really important? That's your call. How important are you? Remember, in order to pan the lasting gold from our streams of stuff, we must be willing to jump in and retrieve the contents. And in order to jump in, you must clear a path. That's what listing is all about. Purge, sweep, dump, sift, sort, and shake down all of your interior goods. You'll find yourself reaping the endless rewards of personal discovery.

The Art of Listmaking

Listmaking is an easy way to turn chaos into order or confusion into poetry. By moving through the pages of this book, you will be selecting and deselecting droves of personal information about yourself. You will be choosing, remembering, favoring, and revealing the core of yourself. In this way, you are actually looking at and arranging unsorted preferences about myriad matters from your entire life. It may not be poetry in motion, but the result of this inventory will give you a sense of place, order, and gratitude for all of the most true, most resonant, and wisest choices you've made. Yes, you are the stuff of great decisions.

Imagine knowing your life's purpose and then being able to live it out fully and completely. What could be more empowering? *More List Your Self* is designed to guide you to self-mastery as you find out more about yourself and your options. List after list will reveal so much of who you are, and in the process you will be able to clarify what you want and figure out how to get there. All you have to do is really scribble and play, but play all the way.

Okay try "List the public figures who have been your strongest role models" and see who shows up. Scour your memory. Don't hold back. Fill in the blanks. Let's see: "John F. Kennedy, Andy Warhol, Leonardo da Vinci, Albert Einstein." The folks on this list are your guiding lights on the road to self-mastery. Now you've got a solid arsenal of inspiration to lead you along the way.

Listing the stuff that makes you *you* is actually a high art, a calling, and a transformative dance. The results are amazing. Not only will you discover information and insights you haven't yet realized about *who you really are,* but you will also build a colorful assortment of life lessons galore—all yours, all valuable. The amount of stuff you have dashing around or hidden inside your cellular brain shelves will determine just how useful and stimulating these life lessons can be.

An inspired and gifted artist once said, "In order to achieve greatness we must first take an inventory of our sensibilities." Sounds like making lists. And once we really start, *boom,* we can zero in, hit our marks, and manifest our dreams. All this from making lists? Yes, all this from piecing together who we are, what we want, where we are going, and what our winning formula is. All this from taking a broad and deep look inside.

How to Use This Book

As with the original *List Your Self,* you can enter the world of listing by jumping in anywhere, anytime. *More List Your Self* is filled to the brim with a variety of list questions to lift your spirits, stimulate your creativity, refocus your mind, and blast you into action. No matter how you are feeling, listmaking is guaranteed to get the wheels of your mind rolling.

If you'd like to start at the beginning of the book, feel free. *More List Your Self* is designed to help you discover the ins and outs of your life experience by giving you many topics to play with. Moving from chapter 1 to chapter 12 makes sense. Start with a warm-up in chapter 1, "Day to Day" to get your list muscles going. This chapter consists of list triggers that examine the rituals and habits that make up your daily life. Then, as you pick up speed, move through the potpourri of rich selections that address your relationships, spirituality, technology, culture, and career.

Or, if you like, you can flip through the pages to find that special chapter that speaks to you right now. Say you are feeling stuck, a little under the weather. Zip through the table of contents and consider settling into chapter 11, "Your Nest" or chapter 10: "Happy Healthy, and Wise." You'll find a litany of list triggers to help you get your balance back. Ready to get into the nitty-gritty of who you are? Turn to chapter 2, "Your Style" or move right into chapter 3, "Big Wisdom." Juggle two chapters, listing between one and the other to explore and shake up your notions about image and what's really important to you. Or do you need to rest and reflect? Take time out and slide into chapter 7, "Sixth Sense." It dishes up list challenges that encourage you to reconnect with your intuition. Or if you want to stretch your imagination, bop right to chapter 12, "Fun, Fantasy, and Adventure." Animate your neurons and play awhile!

Sometimes it's exhilarating to tackle a few lists with great speed and vigor. Choose one that hits the spot and fill in the blanks as fast as you can. Late at night it might be nice to slow down and settle into some of the more provocative lists. Take your time, relax, find the words, and begin.

No matter what your listmaking style,make sure you keep it uninhibited, personal, and true. And don't forget to have fun. You may choose to read your revelations the next day or savor them sometime in the future; it really doesn't matter. So simply jump in and list! Celebrate the gems that come from places long forgotten as you engage and delight in a series of funny, groovy, touching, and profound list portraits. Trust that, as you get to know yourself more and more, the combined wisdom from your listmaking journey will give you everything you need to hit your marks and manifest your dreams.

Chapter I

Day to Day

List your daily rituals that mean the most to you.

List the stuff on your to-do list that is probably a waste of your time and resources.

List the most surprisingly beautiful things you saw today.

List the most persistent and challenging obstacles in your everyday life.

List your personal mottos or inspired words you want to live by.

List the routine things you do that consume most of your time.

List the things you pray for on a daily basis.

I do not pray.
Feels foreign to me.

List the weirdest or most exotic foods you've eaten.

chittlins (fried pig intestines, by accident)

List the things you keep in the house in case of an emergency.

List the most difficult times you've lived through.

List the times in your life you've felt most vulnerable.

List the sounds or thoughts that can keep you up at night.

List the most annoying things you encounter in your work every day.

List the grossest things you've ever had to do.

List the experiences you wish you could do and enjoy over and over again.

List what you do to snap out of a bad mood.

List the things in your daily life that cause you stress.

List the things you do and love on a daily basis.

List what you do to be at peace with yourself, despite the news of the day.

List the occasional song lyrics or pieces of poetry that stream through your mind during the day.

List the things you do that consistently bring you joy.

Chapter 2

Your Style

List the excesses in your life, from possessions to behaviors.

List the things you'd like to do faster.

List the craziest and most inspired things you've ever done.

List the sexually experimental activities you'd like to try.

List the ways you'd like to slow down, if you only could.

List the things you just don't have enough time to do.

List the ways you show off your personal style, from body art to piercings to tattoos—you name it.

List what you like to do when you are alone.

List the typical words people use to describe you.

List the things you've said that you'd like to take back.

List the things that upset you most.

List the ways you've expressed your personal freedom.

List the greatest successes you've achieved.

List the qualities that make you unique.

List the things you were told couldn't be done that you did anyway.

List the ways you take charge.

List the craziest fashions you wore and pranks you pulled off when you were a teenager.

List the surefire ways to melt your lover's heart.

List what you've been known to do when you've lost your inhibitions.

List what talents you'd most like to have.

List the things you do to help others out.

List the things you do to make yourself feel beautiful.

List the way you deceive, fool, or trick others to get your way.

List the areas of your life in which you are truly a beginner.

List the fashions trends you've indulged in.

List the clothing brands you choose that make you feel distinct.

List what gets in the way of you being the person you want to be.

List the illegal things you've done and gotten away with.

List your personal mantras or words to live by.

Chapter 3

Big Wisdom

List the things you need to do to fully achieve your purpose and life dream.

List the people who are doing what you would like to be doing.

List the valuable life lessons you have learned so far.

List the greater powers, human or otherwise, with whom you confide.

List the best teachers, priests, rabbis, and mentors that you've come in contact with.

List what you dream about doing during the last years of your life.

List the things you've learned that you'd like to pass down to the next generation.

List what you love most about being alive.

List the favors you'd like to ask of God or a higher power.

List what you'd do if you had only a few weeks left to live.

List the things you'd actually be willing to die for.

List the times God, fate, or luck seemed to show up and save the day.

List what your life might look like should you actually pull it all together.

List the spiritual pursuits you've undertaken to give your life more meaning.

List the acts you would never do, no matter how much you were paid.

List those key times you've been given a second chance.

List the ways you've paid your dues.

List the times you've been a hero.

List the most remarkable feats of nature, from lightning to shooting stars to the aurora borealis, that you've actually experienced.

Chapter 4

Me.Com

List the situations when your cell phone comes in handy.

List the calls you don't pick up when you see them displayed on your caller ID.

List the computer equipment you really dig.

List your favorite Web sites.

List your favorite things you do on-line.

List the stuff on your hard drive.

List what your own Web site might offer that would be unique and meaningful to the world.

List the things you hope computers won't ever control.

List the Web sites that have become a regular part of your life.

List the nicknames and pseudonyms you use on-line to conceal your identity.

List the ways being on-line has enriched your life.

List some of the frustrations you encounter when you're on-line.

List the weirdest experiences you've had on-line.

List the people you've met on-line.

List the things you could be doing instead of being glued to your computer.

List what you do when your computer freezes, loses data, or won't cooperate.

List the ways modern technology has changed your life.

List the techno gadgets that you can't live without.

List the people from your past who you would like to reconnect with through E-mail.

Chapter 5

CULTURE CLUB

List the historical events you wish never happened.

List the injustices on the planet that trouble you.

List the things you've learned by meeting people from other cultures.

List the things you would change on this planet right now if you had super powers.

List all the people you'd like to be stuck with on a desert island.

List your core contributions to the human race.

List the artwork you'd like to have hanging in your home.

List the news stories that have inspired or influenced your life.

List the TV characters you'd like to know in real life.

List the TV shows you'd like to be a part of.

List some of your most creative expressions, be they singing, dancing, art, or storytelling.

List the famous and not-so-famous minds you'd like to crawl through.

List the songs that have affected or touched you the most.

List the public figures who have been your strongest role models.

List the biggest ways the world has changed since you were a kid.

List the most miraculous inventions and events you've seen in your lifetime.

List the politicians you just don't trust.

List the public places you feel safe visiting.

List the celebrities you'd love to trade places with.

List the contributions you'd like to make to the world.

List the movies that have really defined you.

List the places around the world where you'd like to build your dream home and start a new life.

List the books, magazines, subjects, and articles you are reading at present.

List the freedoms you simply take for granted.

List the countries you have visited that have left a powerful impression on you.

Uganda
Kenya (esp. Nairobi)

List the funniest humans in the past and present.

List the leaders who have changed the world.

List the most creative adventures, trips, and excursions you've taken.

List the books or writings that have influenced your life the most.

Chapter 6

Us

List the people who boost your confidence.

List the members of your family you wish lived closer to you.

List the reasons you don't trust certain people.

List the people who take the wind out of your sails.

List the talents you believe you've inherited from your ancestors.

List the people whose lives you have improved and inspired.

List the people you care about who've moved away.

List the changes you'd like to make in your family.

List the greatest loves of your life.

List the people you include in your core circle.

List the people who would make up your ideal family.

List the people you'd like to smack around, yell at, or simply tell off.

List the most sexually desirable men and women in the world.

List the traits you really crave in a lover.

List the qualities that make up your soul mate.

List the happiest people you know.

List the people you'd like to marry, if it weren't forever.

List the unique powers of being a man.

List the unique powers of being a woman.

List the people you'd like to thank.

List the typical conflicts that happen inside your family.

List the important things you'd like to tell your mother or father.

List the pivotal advice your parents gave you that you actually took.

List the people you need to forgive.

List the people who understand you best.

List the good qualities in your parents you hope you've inherited.

List the people you'd call if you had an emergency.

List those special people you feel really lucky to have met.

List the people you can count on in a crisis, no matter what.

List the people who've done you wrong.

List the people you still know from grammar school or high school.

List the people you wish you weren't so dependent on.

List the unspoken words you want to tell a friend right now.

Chapter 7

SIXTH SENSE

List the times you were in just the right place at the right time.

List the things that scare you the most.

List the times you've really cried your eyes out.

List the things about life that just make no sense at all.

List your typical thoughts when driving on the freeway.

List the most amazing coincidences of your life.

List what you'd like to talk to God about.

List the things you are suspicious of.

List the things you are sick and tired of.

List the ways you've been really lucky.

List the emotions that seem to run your life.

List the sacrifices you've made that have paid off.

List the reasons you would be convinced to sell your soul to the devil.

List the places you believe might ease your mind and soothe your soul.

List what it takes to earn your trust.

List the ways you hide your insecurities.

List the most powerful and life-changing visions you've experienced.

List the personal techniques you practice to empower yourself.

List the things you are grateful for.

Chapter 8

MMMONEY

List the things you love most about your work.

List the jobs or companies you wish would disappear from the face of the earth.

List the many projects you are juggling right now.

List what you want to tell your boss right now.

List your greatest extravagances.

List the ways you've helped others succeed.

List the places you store and hide your money.

List the things you want to do with your nest egg one day.

List the things you believe money can't buy.

List everyone and everything you've given money to for a "good cause."

List the goofiest things you've done to make money.

List the people you still owe money to.

List your luckiest business breaks.

List the things you would never do for money.

List the people and institutions you'd love to sue.

List the stocks and bonds you'd buy if you had a pile of dough.

List the people who you'd like to leave all your money and private treasures to.

List what you'd buy if you won the lottery.

List the contributions you've made at work that have been overlooked.

List the people who have helped you in your career.

List the companies you wish you owned.

List the responsibilities and perks of your "perfect" job.

List the qualities of your ideal work environment.

List what you would do if you suddenly lost everything.

List your greatest investments and assets in life.

Chapter 9

FAVORITE THINGS

List the things you wish you had never bought, owned, or got suckered into thinking you needed.

List your favorite snack foods.

List the things you own that will certainly be passed down from generation to generation.

List the machines you would like to banish if you could.

List the man-made stuff you'd like erased from the planet right now.

List the stuff you've put in your hair.

List the special things you pack when you go on a trip to keep you comfortable and happy.

List the things you avoid because if you indulge in them, you really have no control.

List the man-made things you just can't live without.

List your most treasured possessions.

List the things you wish you had invented.

List the cars you'd like to drive, own, or give to your friends.

List the things you should give away or get rid of that are just taking up space.

List your things that are broken and need repair or attention.

List those special possessions that lift your spirits and make you smile.

List your favorite stores.

List your most extravagant purchases.

List what's in your closet that you just can't part with.

List what it's really time to get rid of.

List the stuff you still store and hold dear from your childhood.

List what's in your basement or attic that you just can't face.

List what you seem to buy over and over again that you don't need.

List the treasures, doodads, and objects you've collected that inspire you.

Chapter 10

HAPPY, HEALTHY, AND WISE

List the biggest catastrophes you've survived.

List the different therapies and treatments you've explored to improve your health.

List when and where you have been your happiest.

List the unconventional health practices that keep you ahead of the game.

List the ways you've abused your body.

List what you see in the mirror that upsets you.

List the special things you treat yourself to when you want to relax.

List the things you loved to do as a kid that you can't do as well anymore.

List your secret remedies to treat a cold, a headache, or a stomachache.

List the things you should have stopped eating long ago, but still occasionally do.

List what you love to do in the nude.

List the things you really need to keep you at your best.

List the many ways you've altered your brain chemistry.

List the things you'd like to change most about your appearance.

List what you could do to immediately simplify your life.

List the wildest health fads you've tried.

List the "imperfections" in yourself that annoy you the most.

List the things you do to defy aging.

List the things you fear most about getting older.

List your plans for having a great and meaningful old age.

List the habits or behaviors of older people you admire.

Chapter II

Your Nest

List the ways your home, street, and neighborhood are extraordinary.

List the causes, charities, and community projects you believe are most worthy.

List what you'd do to improve your home and garden if you had unlimited funds.

List the ways you've contributed to your neighborhood and still do.

List the neighbors who drive you crazy.

List the things you'd like to do to make your home more livable and inviting.

List your favorite places to sit, nestle, and nuzzle.

List the cities you would like to repair or change.

List the stores, shops, and/or malls you would like to add to or eliminate.

List what you could do to make your home and city a better place to live.

List the roads, streets, avenues, and freeways you would like to add to or eliminate to make your town much better.

List what you'd like to see outside your living room window.

List who would suddenly show up if you installed a great swimming pool.

List the "wild" animals you'd keep as pets if you could.

List the animals you wish weren't extinct.

List the plants and trees that you love.

List the bugs, birds, and creatures you can't live without.

List the most beautiful rivers, mountains, and forests you've ever seen.

List the places in nature you'd rather be than where you are right now.

Chapter 12

Fun, Fantasy, and Adventure

List the movies you wish you could escape into.

List who or what you'd like to be reincarnated as.

List the animals you wish roamed free.

List your most frightening phobias, from spiders to dark caves to heights and snakes.

List the ways you escape life and disappear into your secret world.

List the worldly things you wish they would sell at your favorite supermarket.

List the times you've come close to a dangerous or utterly frightening situation.

List the elements of your ultimate "anything goes" weekend.

List the most fantastic places you've spent the night.

List the exotic places you would like to have sex.

List those adventures you've found yourself in that changed or shaped your life.

List the significant cultural events of the past you wish you could have attended.

List the wildest things you've done in public.

List the most remarkable earthly items you'd take to Mars to show off and share with the locals.

List the movie stars you'd like to hang out with.

List the animals you wish you could communicate with.

List the feats you'd attempt, from skydiving to conducting an orchestra, if you just had the courage.

List the poets, artists, writers, and musicians you'd love to have long conversations with.

List the wild places where you'd love to live and disappear from the rat race.

List the outdoor expeditions and journeys from the past you would love to have been a part of.

List how you would feel if you made it to the top of Mt. Everest.